THOMAS CRANE PUBLIC LIBRARY
QUINCY MASS
CITY APPROPRIATION

SNOCROSS

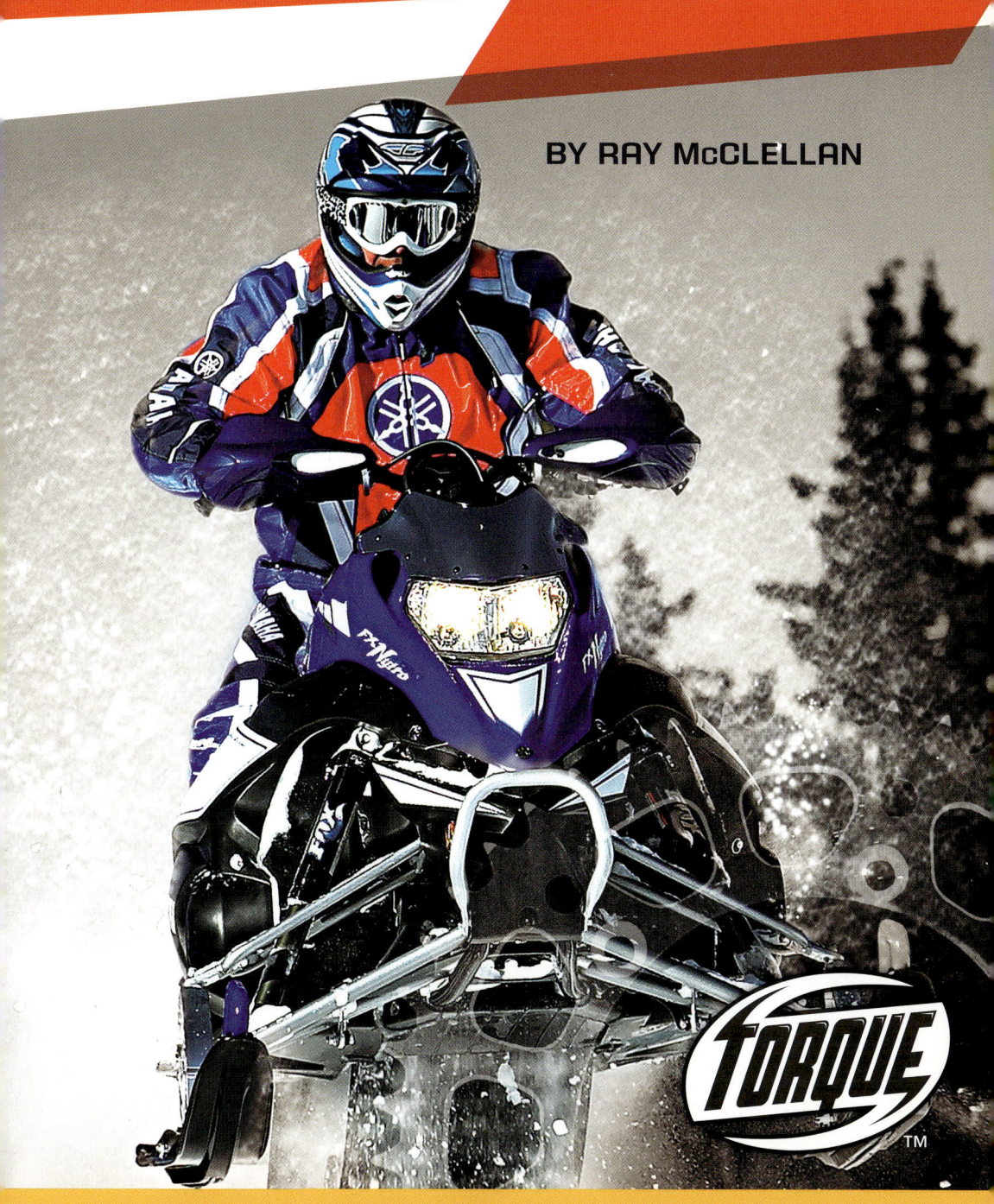

BY RAY McCLELLAN

BELLWETHER MEDIA • MINNEAPOLIS, MN

Are you ready to take it to the extreme? Torque books thrust you into the action-packed world of sports, vehicles, and adventure. These books may include dirt, smoke, fire, and dangerous stunts.

WARNING: Read at your own risk.

This edition first published in 2008 by Bellwether Media.

No part of this publication may be reproduced in whole or in part without written permission of the publisher. For information regarding permission, write to Bellwether Media Inc., Attention: Permissions Department, Post Office Box 19349, Minneapolis, MN 55419.

Library of Congress Cataloging-in-Publication Data
McClellan, Ray.
 Snocross / by Ray McClellan.
    p. cm. — (Torque : action sports)
 Summary: "Amazing photography accompanies engaging information about Snocross. The combination of high-interest subject matter and light text is intended for students in grades 3 through 7"—Provided by publisher.
 Includes bibliographical references and index.
 ISBN-13: 978-1-60014-143-0 (hardcover : alk. paper)
 ISBN-10: 1-60014-143-9 (hardcover : alk. paper)
 1. Snocross—Juvenile literature. I. Title.
GV856.85.M33 2008
796.9—dc22   2007040557

Text copyright © 2008 by Bellwether Media.
SCHOLASTIC, CHILDREN'S PRESS, and associated logos are trademarks and/or registered trademarks of Scholastic Inc. Printed in the United States of America.

CONTENTS

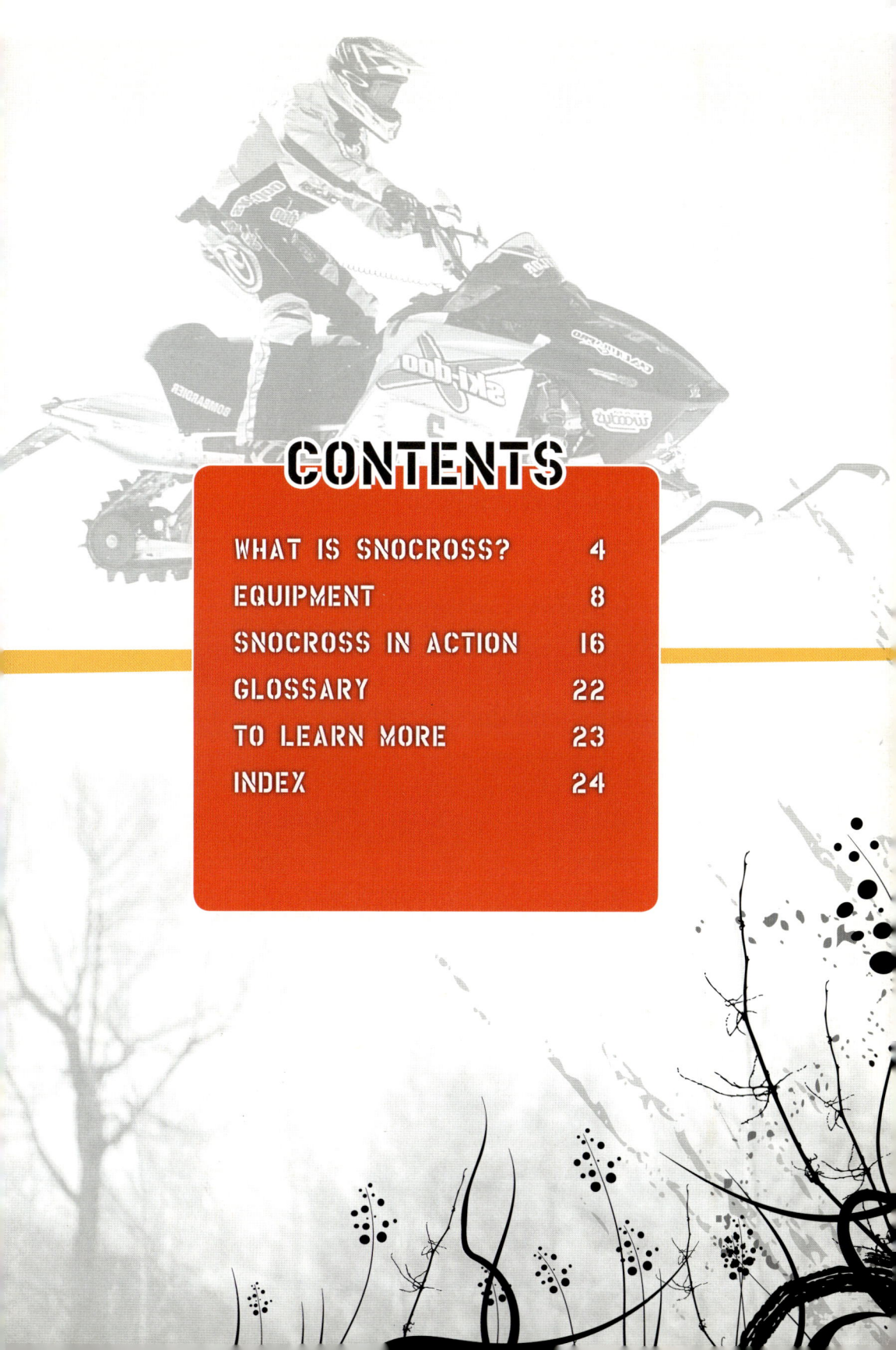

WHAT IS SNOCROSS? 4
EQUIPMENT 8
SNOCROSS IN ACTION 16
GLOSSARY 22
TO LEARN MORE 23
INDEX 24

WHAT IS SNOCROSS?

When it starts snowing, snocross riders get ready to race. Snocross is the sport of racing snowmobiles on specially designed courses filled with thrilling jumps and daring turns.

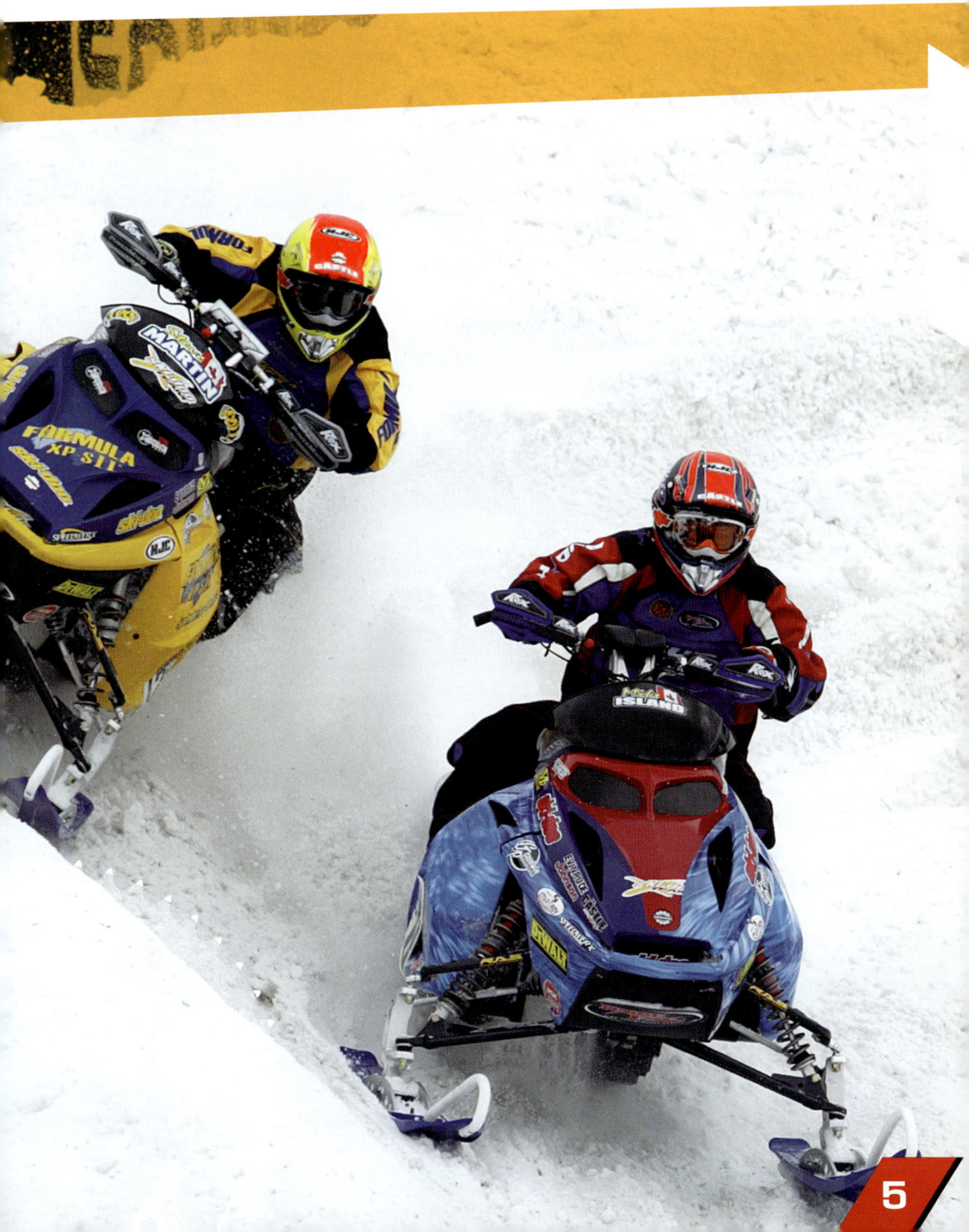
FORMULA
MARTIN
ISLAND
HJC

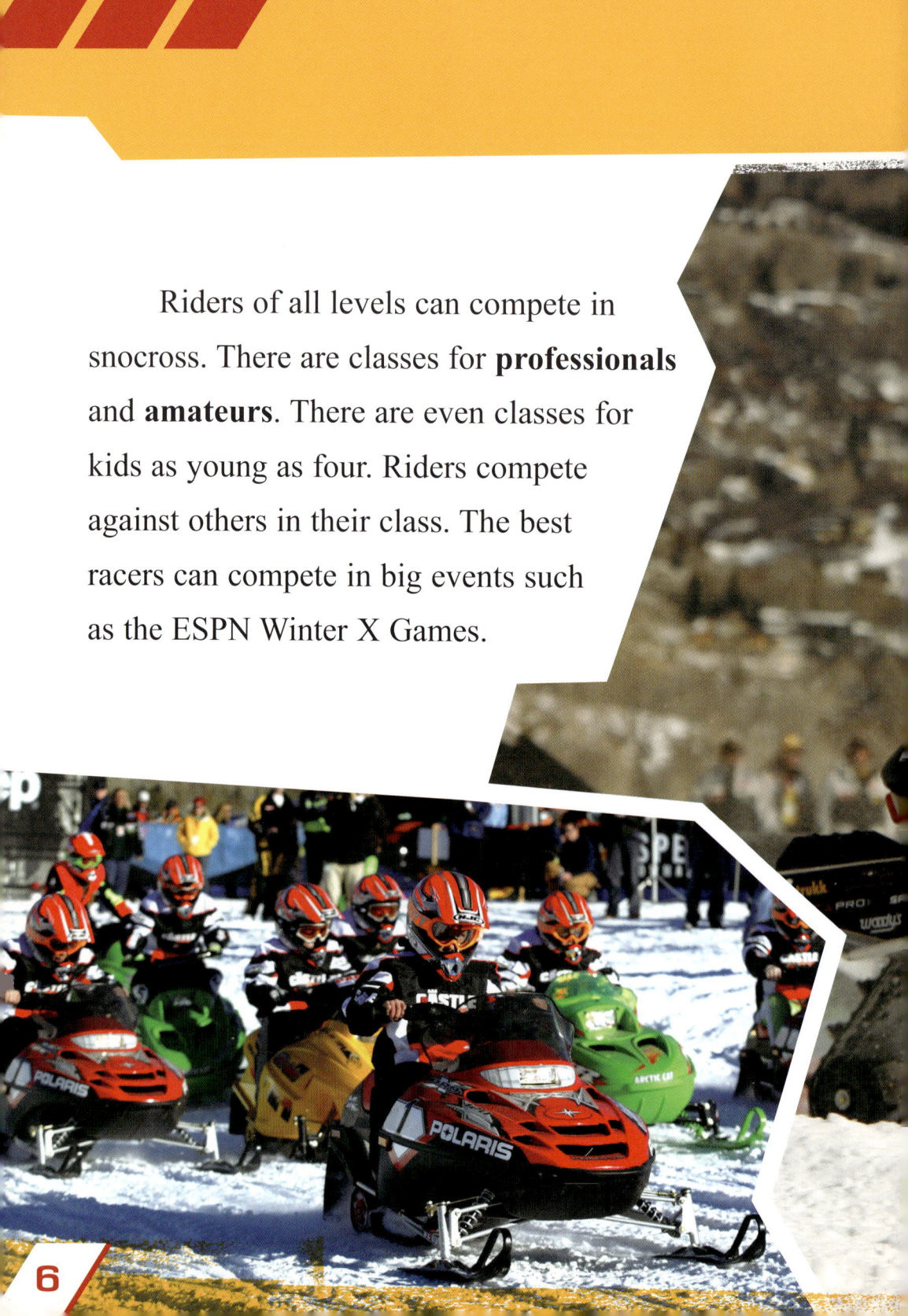

Riders of all levels can compete in snocross. There are classes for **professionals** and **amateurs**. There are even classes for kids as young as four. Riders compete against others in their class. The best racers can compete in big events such as the ESPN Winter X Games.

fast fact

Snocross was the first motorized sport to be included in the X Games (summer or winter). It first appeared in 1998.

7

EQUIPMENT

All snowmobiles, or **sleds**, have some basic features. Sleds have a pair of skis in the front and a **track** in the back. The pair of skis in the front connects to handlebars. Turning the handlebars controls the direction of the skis. The track is under the back of the sled. The track is a large belt that moves around a set of wheels. Sharp pieces of metal called **studs** are attached to the track. The studs dig into the snow and provide **traction**.

Fast Fact

Snowmobile engines are measured in cubic centimeters (cc). Snocross engines can be as small as 100cc or as large as 1,000cc. Big engines give sleds lots of speed. They can go more than 100 miles (161 kilometers) per hour!

Snocross sleds are specially designed for racing. Their frame, or **chassis**, is lighter and stronger than the frame of a regular snowmobile. Powerful racing engines can get these machines moving at very high speeds. Top sleds can reach maximum speeds in just four seconds.

11

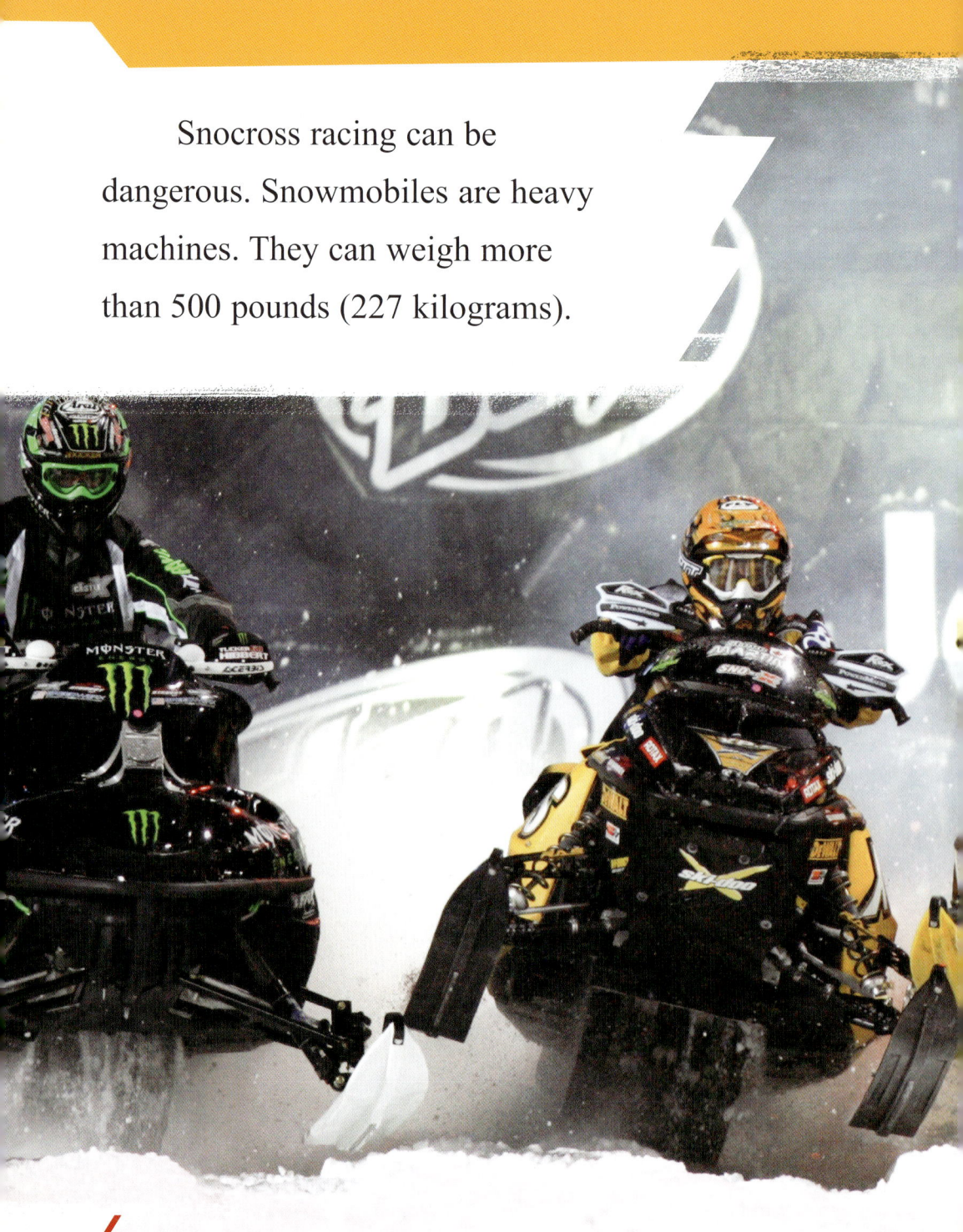

Snocross racing can be dangerous. Snowmobiles are heavy machines. They can weigh more than 500 pounds (227 kilograms).

13

14

Crashes can be violent. Racers protect themselves with **body armor**, helmets, and face shields. They also wear a special cord attached to their wrist and to the snowmobile. If a racer falls off, the cord pulls free from the snowmobile. When that happens, the sled's engine stops.

SNOCROSS IN ACTION

Snocross races are noisy, fun, and packed with action. Between 20 and 30 sleds fight it out on a half-mile (0.8-kilometer) course. Sleds often bump and scrape into each other on the sharp turns. A course is filled with hills and jumps. Sled engines roar as they speed up the hills. Riders and their huge machines soar high in the air as they launch off jumps at high speeds.

The first seconds of a race are critical. Racers fight for the **holeshot**. The first sled to get through the first turn has a big advantage. The rider can block other sleds from taking the lead. The winner of the holeshot wins the race about half the time.

Fast Fact

Small hills in a snocross course are called moguls. Several moguls close together are called whoops. A rider needs intense concentration and skill to maneuver the whoops.

20

The holeshot is just the first step to winning a race. Racers must hit every turn and jump just right. A small mistake can send a rider smashing into a snow bank or off the course. The rider who can hold the lead will take the checkered flag and victory!

GLOSSARY

amateur—someone who competes in a sport for fun rather than for money

body armor—a strong, body-fitting piece of plastic and foam that snocross riders wear underneath their clothes to protect them during crashes

chassis—the metal frame of a snowmobile

holeshot—the position of being first to reach the course's first turn

professional—someone who is paid to compete in a sport

sled—another term for a snowmobile

studs—metal spikes attached to the track to allow even better grip on the snow

track—the large belt that wraps around a snowmobile's wheels and provides grip on snow and ice

traction—the grip of a machine on a racing surface; a snowmobile's track gives it good traction on snow.

TO LEARN MORE

AT THE LIBRARY
Budd, E.S. *Snowmobiles*. Chanhassen, Minn.: Child's World, 2004.

Doeden, Matt. *Snowmobiles*. Mankato, Minn.: Capstone, 2005.

Maurer, Tracy. *Snocross*. Vero Beach, Fla.: Rourke, 2003.

ON THE WEB
Learning more about snocross is as easy as 1, 2, 3.

1. Go to www.factsurfer.com
2. Enter "snocross" into search box.
3. Click the "Surf" button and you will see a list of related web sites.

With factsurfer.com, finding more information is just a click away.

INDEX

1998, 7
amateurs, 6
body armor, 15
chassis, 10
checkered flag, 21
classes, 6
course, 4, 17, 19, 21
crashes, 15
cubic centimeters, 9
engines, 9, 10, 15, 17
handlebars, 8
holeshot, 18, 21
moguls, 19
professionals, 6
safety, 15
skis, 8
studs, 8
track, 8
traction, 8
whoops, 19
X Games, 6, 7

The images in this book are reproduced through the courtesy of: Yamaha Motor Corporation, cover; Markus Paulsen/Shazamm/ESPN Images, pp. 5, 9, 10, 21; Bakke/Shazamm/ESPN Images, p. 6; Scott Clarke/Shazamm/ESPN Images, pp. 7, 11 (bottom), 18, 19 (top), 20; Mike Roth/Shazamm/ESPN Images, p. 11 (top); Allen Kee/Shazamm/ESPN Images, pp. 12-13; Pierre Catellier/Shazamm/ESPN Images, pp. 14, 16, 19 (bottom); C Stein/Shazamm/ESPN Images, p. 15; ESPN Images, p. 17.

CC

THOMAS CRANE PUBLIC LIBRARY
3 1641 0082 4215 2

Central Children's

FEB 2009